For Sarah Odedina, a very special mother hen indeed – S.G.

To Ken W.M. You're a good egg! – J.N.

Bloomsbury Publishing, London, Berlin and New York

First published in Great Britain in 1999 by Bloomsbury Publishing Plc
36 Soho Square, London, W1D 3QY

This paperback edition first published in April 2000

Text copyright © Sally Grindley 1999
Illustrations copyright © Jill Newton 1999
The moral rights of the author and illustrator have been asserted

A CIP catalogue record of this book is available from the British Library

ISBN 978 0 7475 4669 6

Designed by Dawn Apperley

Printed in China by South China Printing Co., Dongguan City, Guangdong

5 7 9 8 6 4

All papers used by Bloomsbury Publishing Plc are natural, recyclable products made from
wood grown in well-managed forests. The manufacturing processes conform to the
environmental regulations of the country of origin.

www.bloomsbury.com

Where are my Chicks?

Sally Grindley and Jill Newton

BLOOMSBURY

LONDON BERLIN NEW YORK

Mother Hen couldn't find her chicks.
"My chicks, my chicks!
I've lost my chicks!" she cried.

"We'll help you find them," said the bee and the frog and the donkey and the pig.
"You should take better care of your chicks," said Mother Goose.

"Here's one," said the bee.
"Oh, my little chick, I missed you so,"
said Mother Hen.

"That's one," said the wise owl.

"Here's one," said the frog.
"Oh, where have you been, my little sunshine?"
said Mother Hen.

"That's two,"
said the wise owl.

"Here's one," said the donkey.
"You had me so worried,
my little sausage,"
said Mother Hen.

"That's three," said the wise owl.

"There's one here," said the pig.
"Come to me, my precious pet," said Mother Hen.

"That's four," said the wise owl.

"Here's another," said the rabbit.

"That's five,"
said the wise owl.

"And another," said the goat.

"That's six," said the wise owl.

"And another," said the sheep.

"That's seven,"
said the wise owl.

"And one more," said the dragonfly.

"That makes eight," said the wise owl.

"But I only had four!" said Mother Hen.

"My goslings! I've lost my goslings!" cried Mother Goose.

"You should take better care of your goslings,"
said Mother Hen.

"Here they are all safe and sound."

"Now where are my little bundles of joy?"
said Mother Hen.

"Come here, my poppets, come to mummy."

Acclaim for this book

'The humour will appeal to adults sharing the story, and it will also provide a fun start in the learning of numeracy skills.' *The Bookseller*

'This gently ironic story is laid out in double page spreads in bold opaque colours, giving it a modern feel for all the old style farm setting.' *Books For Keeps*

'The illustrations are big and bright, with just the right amount of detail to hold a child's attention.' *Manchester Evening News*